ON THE MOVE

TRAINS

**For a free color catalog describing Gareth Stevens'
list of high-quality books and multimedia programs,
call 1-800-542-2595 (USA) or 1-800-461-9120 (Canada).
Gareth Stevens Publishing's Fax: (414) 225-0377.
See our catalog, too, on the World Wide Web:
http://gsinc.com**

Library of Congress Cataloging-in-Publication Data

Stickland, Paul.
    Trains / Paul Stickland.
        p. cm. — (On the move)
    Includes index.
    Summary: Introduces, in brief text and illustrations, various
types of trains and their uses.
    ISBN 0-8368-2154-8 (lib. bdg.)
    1. Railroads—Trains—Juvenile literature. [1. Railroads—Trains.]
I. Title. II. Series: Stickland, Paul. On the move.
TF550.S85 1998
625.2—dc21   98-3349

This North American edition first published in 1998 by
Gareth Stevens Publishing
1555 North RiverCenter Drive, Suite 201
Milwaukee, Wisconsin 53212 USA

© 1991 by Paul Stickland.
Produced by Mathew Price Ltd.,
The Old Glove Factory, Bristol Road,
Sherborne, Dorset DT9 4HP, England.
Additional end matter © 1998
by Gareth Stevens, Inc.

Gareth Stevens series editor: Dorothy L. Gibbs
Editorial assistant: Diane Laska

Printed in Hong Kong

1 2 3 4 5 6 7 8 9 02 01 00 99 98

TRAINS

Paul Stickland

Gareth Stevens Publishing
MILWAUKEE

Old trains were pulled by steam engines.

They burned coal to make the steam.

The red pusher on the front of this
early American steam engine is called
a cowcatcher.

A trolley car is like a bus, except it goes through town on rails set into the roads.

This train has about one hundred heavy coal cars.

It takes four powerful diesel-electric engines to pull them.

This special train can climb mountains
through slippery ice and snow.

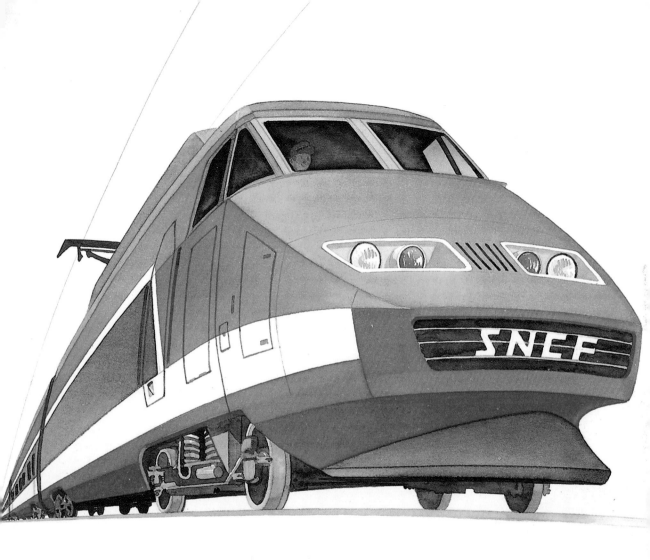

The fastest train in the world can go
180 miles (290 kilometers) an hour.

switch engine   milk tank car

flatcar

coal car   hopper car

oil tank car

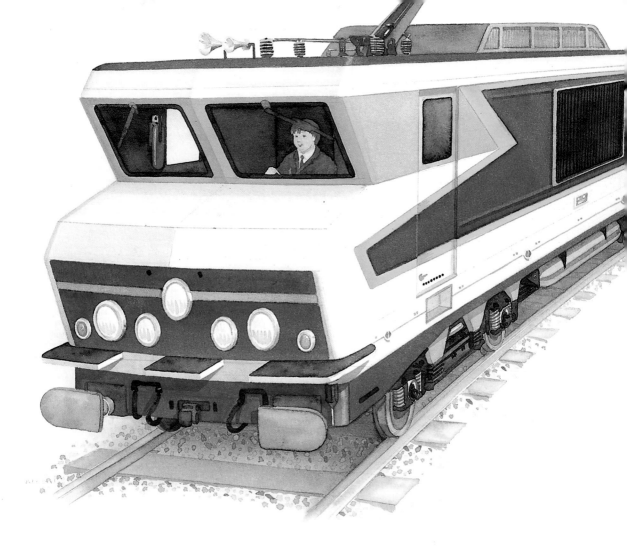

One powerful electric engine can pull
this long train of cars.

GLOSSARY

coal — a black solid substance found deep in the ground. It is burned to make heat.

cowcatcher — the pointed part on the front of a train engine that pushes things off the track.

diesel-electric — having both a diesel engine (an engine that uses air to burn fuel) and an electric generator.

hopper — a train car with a floor that slopes down to a door for emptying its load.

switch engine — a train engine that moves railroad cars from one track to another.

trolley car — a rail car that can go on a road or street and uses electric power from wires connected to the top of it.

INDEX